Sleeping with Holiness

Daura Jones and Daphne Parker

Inspiring Voices®
A Service of Guideposts

References with Greek meanings are taken from: Thayer and Smith "The NAS
Greek Lexicon", 1999, http://www.biblestudytools.com/lexicons/greek/nas/ (7,
June, 2012) (Koimao, Strongs #2837, Osphys, Strong's #3751, Hupotasso, Strong's
#5293, Agape, Strong's #26, Phileo, Strong's#5368,Meno, Strong's #3306)

References with Hebrew meanings are taken from Thayer and Smith "The NAS
Old Testament Hebrew Lexicon", 1999, http://www.biblestudytools.com/lexicons/
hebrew/nas/chayah.html (7, June, 2012) (Restoreth, Strong's #2421)

English Definitions taken from The American Heritage® New Dictionary of
Cultural Literacy, Third Edition Copyright © 2005 by Houghton Mifflin
Company. Published by Houghton Mifflin Company, (7, June, 2012)

Unless otherwise noted, Scripture quotations are (KJV) and (NIV) taken from the http://biblegateway.com.
Copyright © 1995-2010, The Zondervan Corporation. All rights Reserved.

Inspiring Voices books may be ordered through booksellers or by contacting:
Inspiring Voices
1663 Liberty Drive
Bloomington, IN 47403
www.inspiringvoices.com
1-(866) 697-5313

ISBN: 978-1-4624-0220-5 (sc)
ISBN: 978-1-4624-0219-9 (e)
Library of Congress Control Number: 2012942896

Printed in the United States of America
Inspiring Voices rev. date: 07/26/2012

Contents

Preface

Why is carnality ruling the lifestyles of Christians? In the body of Christ today, there are many habits and attitudes that need to be addressed and removed from believer's hearts. Whether we are a pastor or a deacon, a mother or a father, a faithful employee, a brother or a sister, a daughter or a son, we are held accountable for our own actions. Through the three principles of love, believers need to exercise their power to instruct, correct, and embrace others.

There are personal challenges and emotional burdens a believer must overcome as he or she begins to walk closer towards destiny. Believers must understand that sin begins inside the body of man (heart, mind & soul) working its way into the body of Christ. However, as believers grow intimate with Christ, the weight of iniquity dissipates out of his or her life. The information provided in **Sleeping with Holiness** is essentially for believers to make the necessary choice to strengthen their relationship with God and to live disciplined lives.

Dedication

First and foremost, we express our earnest thanks to the Holy Trinity, (Father, Son & Holy Ghost) for giving us the strength, peace and agreement in writing **Sleeping with Holiness**. We would like to give honor to our parents, Moses and Mary, children Jasmine and Tarbree, and our brother, Darren.

Thank you all for reading **Sleeping with Holiness**. We pray that the truth be revealed to you and may God endow you with power to move into the next season of your life!

Introduction

The hour has come for God to purge out filthiness and perfect the Body of Christ for the near end times. As wicked as the world may seem right now, it is going to get a lot worse in the coming years. Matthew 24:12 states, "... *because iniquity shall abound, the love of many shall wax cold.*" Therefore, it is God's intention for believers to follow the thelema (individual) will for his or her life. Philippians 2:13 states,"*For it is God which worketh in you both to will and to do of his good pleasure.*"

The Lord has mandated the two of us to go out and to inform every believer, including those fallen from their place in Christ Jesus, about the detriments of living without His holiness. 2 Peter 2:21 states, "*For it had been better for them not to have known the way of righteousness, than, after they have known it, to turn from the holy commandment delivered unto them.*"

As believers, we are held accountable to the knowledge we have attained in Christ Jesus (Philippians 3:16). Every hidden and overt sin must be placed on the altar so our spiritual gifts can be used appropriately and not be centered on selfish gains in this dying world. Believers are to walk with integrity and obedience, not in personal victory.

This is the time for the people of God to uphold their position in God's holiness so we might not fall away from our faith and lead others into destruction of everlasting punishment. Without holiness, no one shall see God. Time is running out! Holiness must come back (in our teaching and lifestyles) into the Body of Christ before it's too late.

Sleeping with Holiness will draw believers into a deeper intimacy with God. Then, we will be able to hear from God, obey His commands, and trust in Him without wavering.

In order to be intimate with God, there has to be a consistent practice of prayer, meditation, reading and obeying God's Word, walking by faith, resting in spirit, and submitting to the love of God. When one encounters daily intimacy with God, one completely gives up carnal desires and cease from sins.

Holiness brings faith that manifests the glory of God to keep us away from unclean spirits. Believers must carry out what they believe in the Word of God and trust God to bring it to pass.

Many Christians are deceived by false doctrines and selfish gains. These are the two lethal weapons that the antichrist employs in the hearts and minds of believers. False doctrines lead believers to deception. The spirit of pride, doubt, and ignorance open the doors to deception. If believers become entangle with their own pleasures, they can become distracted in their hearts which makes it difficult to follow the way of righteousness.

The Bible speaks about apostasy in 2 Thessalonians 2:3 stating, "*Let no man deceive you by any means: for that day shall not come, except there comes a falling away first, and that man of sin be revealed, the son of perdition.*"

Men have developed strange (false) doctrines that are now accepted in the church. Yet instead of rebuking the dogma, some believers embraced the language and lifestyle therein causing dissension and division.

If the body of Christ continues to allow unsacred practices to enter into its place of worship, then the Church as a whole is in jeopardy of falling into apostasy. We cannot limit ourselves or reduce our time spent in quality devotion to God and in meditating on the Word since this is where we gain insight into the power of His might and discernment between truth and deception.

There are many believers who have attended services for many years, yet their minds have never been transformed to fulfill the perfect will of God. As a result, they begin to partake in wickedness which may end up in apostasy. They do not realize where overt sin may lead. But in the New Covenant, there is the hope with the blood of the Lamb and baptism: washing away sins, dying to self and everlasting resurrection.

We must begin to examine ourselves using the Word of Truth. After truth is revealed, it becomes a witness to the righteous heart in us. Our hearts will begin to trust and submit to God to develop an intimacy with Him so as to fulfill the character of holy and royal priesthoods in Christ Jesus. When we surrender to the intimacy with God, it manifests in our lifestyles, our conversations, in our dreams, when we lie down and when we rise up.

Holiness is distinctive, with implications of being set apart for the commitment to God. It's not enough to just say no to unclean living. Within the process of manifesting holiness, we are graced with the power to choose to let go of our "self" (old ways and habits). The proof is in the pudding, which is, showing in our lifestyle that we have let go of self.

If the Church will begin to sleep with holiness, then the glory of God can infiltrate the lives of every believer. There will be more healing, more deliverance, more miracles, more love, and more power to sustain salvation and God's righteousness. When believers commit to letting go of former thoughts and habits, God will step in to guide them to that next phase of purpose in their life. Faithful believers must surrender their hearts willingly, act in true humility and maintain patience as they wait on God.

While enduring our cross, we must stand still without stagnating in emotions or questioning circumstances. We cannot allow our emotions and thoughts to overtake us. Often, believers step out of the will of God and begin to question what their next move should be. They begin to step out of God's will by appeasing their flesh. When doubt occurs, it minimizes trust in the power of God. We must uphold our faith, trust God and follow Christ's example of endless righteousness.

Holiness teaches us when to wait, when to move, when to speak, when to keep quiet, when to say no to ungodliness and how to control strong and compelling emotions such as sexual desires or covetousness. Holiness shows us how to bear fruits and remain faithful in our walk with God.

Holiness is the result of sanctification by God which freely justifies us. When we are justified by God, we can begin our daily walk in the Spirit. When we walk in the Spirit, we remain in God's perfect will for our lives. We begin to take authority over the works of the flesh.

Holiness brings a concrete manifestation of keeping God's Word close to our hearts. David said, "*Thy word have I hid in mine heart that I might not sin against thee.*" (Psalm 119:11) This means the Word of God will keep us holy. It will keep us from giving up and falling into temptation. As we walk each day with the Word of God in our minds, it will preserve our hearts to worship God without apathy and stagnation. If this is the case, sin should not be an alternative because we are in the right alignment with God's perfect will for our lives.

We should dedicate our whole lives to divine worship and withdraw ourselves from worldly pleasures such as going to a bar and gambling at a casino. Those of us who have a greater degree of separation from carnal deeds yearn for a deeper place in God. As we move to a deeper place in God, there will be seasons when we are set apart from people, places, and things. When we go through hardships and crisis, we may continue to exercise our faith in God and not depend on drugs, sex, or alcohol.

When the natural body sleeps, it goes into the anabolic state: a process of restoration, rejuvenation and repair of the body and its cells. So just as the natural body needs restoration, the spirit must also be restored, rejuvenated, and repaired from the cells and heartaches in life. The nature of this spiritual process of rest is similar to natural rest, except that it is deeper and more profound. The body of Christ must go into a spiritual rest to prepare for a higher relationship in and with God; spiritual rest is a necessity to allow restoration of the heart and mind.

The Greek word for "sleep" is "Koimao", which means to calm, quiet or be still (Thayer and Smith, Strongs#2837). Spiritual sleep allows the work of God's hand to establish the pattern of our lives while we are being still in our emotions and habits. This will allow God to order our steps. God has to reboot our spirit so to speak in order to fill our heart and position our feet back on track for the next journey of our lives. While sleeping (being still and calm), the fruit of the Spirit will manifest itself to guide us in every step that we take. The fruit of the Spirit allows us to let go of the way we used to do certain things. It will mature our character so we can bear all things.

Sometimes we may lose the battle because we experience the death of a loved one, marital separation, and/or the loss of job or home. However, how we choose to go through these trials will draw us to or away from righteousness.

The trials and tribulations we go through should teach us how to be stronger and more reliant on God, in all aspects of our lives, ministries, marriages, and relationships. We are not excluded from challenges in life when we commit to daily worship to God. However, we can overcome these challenges and obstacles by relying on the strength of God and not on our own strength. When sleeping with holiness, we can pass through the trials of life and not be burned (see

Daniel 3:19-30). We can release our burdens and let go of anger, anxiety, hurt and pain. We can give it all to God.

God commanded times of rest for the land in Leviticus 25:5. Today, God is commanding us to rest for a time of edifying, correction, and uninterrupted fellowship. God served as a model for this when He rested on the seventh day from his work of creation (read Genesis 2). Peace dwelled within God, just as peace dwells in us through Christ Jesus. He pronounced His work to be excellent, just as He wants to pronounce His excellence in us. Believers have been given the tools to protect and develop a new character of holiness. It is crucial to keep one's spirit, mind and body reposed in holiness. "*For God hath not called us unto uncleanness, but unto holiness.*" (I Thessalonians 4:7).

Chapter 1

Enter into the Resting Place

"Come unto me, all ye that labor and are heavy laden, and I will give you rest; Take my yoke upon you, and learn of me; for I am meek and lowly in heart: and you shall find rest unto your souls. For my yoke is easy, and my burden is light."

Matthew 11:28-30

Spiritual rest is a period that occurs during a specific season. This season prepares you to be positioned into a new place in God. There may be times when there is no movement in your ministry or when times in your life seem to be stale. However, rest is a time of mind shifting that will reveal greater depth of your purpose. It is a time for uninterrupted fellowship with God so we can see the truth and understand our purpose on earth. Rest is a function of our hearts, minds, and bodies that God requires us to undergo in order to fulfill complete restoration. A continued cycle of restoration is essential so we do not become stagnant in our purpose.

It is easy for us as believers to lose our vision of God's sovereignty when our burdens are so pressing upon our souls or when we become conditioned to our habits. In biblical times, the Jews were accustomed to keeping the letter of the law and refused to embrace the refined concept of holiness-through Jesus Christ. Jesus began to speak to the Jews, who were heavily burdened, about their traditions of keeping up with the Mosaic laws. In Matthew 11:28-30, Jesus was simply telling them to let go and be free from the burdens of old customs and religion. Are you tired of the void in your worship service? Are you burned out of religion? This rest is for you! Exchange your burdens with Jesus' burdens. It's easier to bear.

We should be open to opportunities for holiness to manifest in a deeper capacity. There may be opportunities for you to demonstrate love, comfort others, teach, exhort, or preach, both on a corporate and an individual level. These are all so desperately needed within the body of Christ. These opportunities edify believers to be stronger vessels to carry Christ to the unbelievers. We don't want to be burdened down by unnecessary labors and miss the move of God. We need a cleansing. When we enter into a resting place, we are washed, corrected, and strengthened from the things we endure. Holiness demands a paradigm shift every now and then to purify us from generational curses, negative perspectives, sicknesses, old fables, and the forbidden fruit of opinions, people, places, and circumstances.

God wants the body of Christ to be diligent in resting so we will be able to bear one another's burdens. Diligence builds character so we may be able to train others for service. If we rest just a little while longer, God will provide us with instructions and direct our paths in righteousness. He knows all we are facing right now and all we will face in the future. There is no time to turn back to Egypt (world/ former places). All we have to do is enter the resting place of God that keeps us in peace allotted by grace. If God brought you out, then keep going forward.

Enter the resting place with your mind, spirit, and body concentrated on God. When circumstances contribute to the constraints of heavy burdens, your ability and perceptions are limited, which, oppresses the mind and spirit. This can produce certain illnesses in the physical body. Before we go any further, you must recognize and overcome struggles found within the three-fold structure of man: mind, spirit, and body.

Transformation of the Mind

Satan tries to penetrate the soul of man by tempting the mind through the lust of the flesh, the lust of the eyes, and the pride of life. Satan uses the mind as a battleground to torment and deceive believers, but the Word of God will shield your mind with instructions on keeping peace. The mind of Christ was filled with peace because of his knowledge and confidence in God. His obedience was subject to the will of God, that it might glorify God's holy name in every area of his life.

The kingdom of God works in the minds of men. Therefore, our minds must be renewed by the Word of God. Satan's tactical plan to destroy our souls is by deviation of the mind, with patterns of evil thoughts and vain imaginations.

Delays, setbacks, defeats, sickness, and diseases are part of Satan's stumbling blocks to hinder our minds from focusing on God.

If you want to win the battles of your mind and fight off the temptations of evil thoughts, then you must experience true transformation by the Word of God. For many years, we were taught falsely that the soul and spirit are one. The soul contacts the intellect and mental abilities of man. The soul is part of man that reasons and thinks. The soul is a part of the mind where Satan can dominate if not changed. The mind is a battlefield of true and false thinking. Our mentality may appear to be all together (focused in our ministries, in our finances, and in our businesses). However, if our minds have not been transformed, then we will fall into our own demise.

We must understand that the soul is the sphere of activity where Satan operates and makes his appeal to the affections and emotions of man. The Greek word for mind is osphýs (pronounced os-foos) (Strong's #3751). It means reproductive area or generative power. The mind can generate divine power if it is transformed by God's Word. In contrast, the mind can generate negative power if it is filled with unclean thoughts and unclean images.

Our minds lose holy power when our creative capacity has been compromised with images of Harry Potter or pornography instead of images of the cross. The Word of God restores the mind from evil seeds that have been planted since we were born. In Psalm 23:3, David says: "*He restoreth my soul*". The Hebrew word translated "restoreth" is said to mean "*to preserve alive, let live.*" (*Strong's #2421*)

At no time had David lost his salvation, but there were times when his affections and desires were turned from the Lord, as with his sin with Bathsheba (2 Samuel 11:1-4). It was the mercy and sovereignty of God preserved (and let live) David's soul from his afflicted pit-fall.

We often worry about issues we have no control over. When issues intensify in our lives and consume our thoughts, we might find an easy route of pacification by material gains or turning to people who have no interest in our destiny. We must operate with a higher faith when we experience intense pressure in the world. Until we allow the mind of Christ to rule our thoughts, we will continue to come to conclusions based on carnal reasoning and not on spiritual truth. In the resting place, there will be times when you may experience weariness or hopelessness in your mind. The weariness of your mind will cause you to struggle with what God has already spoken over your life.

We must be on guard and sound in our minds. The Word of God promises that peace will overflow when you keep your mind on Christ Jesus (Philippians 4:7/ Isaiah 26:3). Friends, "*Therefore gird up the loins of your mind, be sober, and hope to the end for the grace that is to be brought unto you at the revelation of Jesus Christ;*" (1 Peter 1:13). Do not indulge your mind (soul) with unclean thoughts that will distract you from receiving your inheritance (peace and joy) in Christ Jesus. We cannot become new creatures in Christ Jesus if our thoughts are consumed with idols of money, power, titles, lust, and negative perceptions. What looks good to you is not always good for you. If you are not sure if the thoughts you consume are healthy or not, then ask yourself this question when: "Can this thought manifest glorification to God when the work is in fruition?"

Spirit of Man

Holiness begins in the heart of man and produces a perfect heart. When an unsaved person accepts Jesus as his Lord and Savior, his spirit becomes regenerated. It takes on a new life and a new nature (2 Corinthians 5:17). God begins to reveal hidden truths to those who have been saved by his Spirit to perfect his purpose in them. As we progress in our spiritual walk, holiness begins to penetrate truth in our hearts for right living. The heart of man is convicted when unclean spirits attempt to enter. We will begin to see and hear the voice of God more clearly. God has given us the breastplate of righteousness to protect our hearts from the fiery darts of the enemy. It is righteousness that keeps our heart with integrity, purity of life, sincerity, and devotion to God. Righteousness protects the heart from yielding to the cares of the world. It keeps our hearts from losing faith as we focus on our purpose on earth.

God's grace and mercy brings us into the resting place, but we have to choose to remain. Remain in that place until you hear God's voice directing and guiding you. It becomes a danger when you leave the resting place. Adam and Eve left the resting place. God gave them a perfect world, but they were drawn by the lust of the flesh, the lust of the eyes, and the pride of life which led them out of holiness. They've lost their fellowship with God, their lordship over the earth, immortality, and incorruptible knowledge.

The children of Israel left the resting place. They complained, murmured, and practiced self-will to worship a golden calf. Because of their disobedience, their nine day journey turned into a forty year voyage. Most of that generation died in the wilderness because of their unbelief.

King Saul left the resting place. He offered an unlawful sacrifice to the Lord. He sought his own will instead of seeking God's will. He lost his place as the king of Israel.

There are so many other examples in the Bible of what happens to people who left the resting place. Our hearts need to be guarded so we can remain in the rest of God. Some of us today may have left the resting place, but get back into your place and take hold to righteous living. Don't let your labor be in vain because "*he that shall endure unto the end, the same shall be saved*" (Matthew 24:13).

The Body—Temple of the Holy Ghost

"*Do you not know that your bodies are temples of the Holy Spirit, who is in you, whom you have received from God? You are not your own;*" (1 Corinthians 6:19) Our bodies are the temple of the Holy Ghost. It is the physical body of man that has the ability to contact the world using five senses: hearing, touching, seeing, smelling, and tasting. We are ordered by God to use all our being to glorify Him, worship Him and bring others to Him. However, we are not exempted from the afflictions of our bodies. If our bodies are not rested, then they become vulnerable to unnecessary burdens such as stress. Stress can lead to strokes, mental crisis, depression, fatigue, memory loss, increased respiratory rate, gastrointestinal problems, dizziness, muscle tension, and even death.

Stress is an easy distraction the enemy uses to deter us from our purpose of worshiping and fellowshipping with God. The enemy uses such physical afflictions as a weapon to shake our faith and to doubt God. We cannot allow the enemy to dominate our physical nature based on a temporary state of being. God has given us authority over sickness and diseases. We have the power to discipline our bodies.

1 Thessalonians 5:23b says, "*May your whole spirit, soul and body be kept blameless at the coming of our Lord Jesus Christ.*" One of the rudiments in God's plan is to bring sanctification and holiness, not only to our soul and spirit, but also to our body. The Holy Spirit (the active Person of the Triumvirate on earth) is ready to give life to our mortal bodies.

God desires our obedience and submission to keep our bodies pure from sin. We want to eat hamburgers and greasy fries all week, but God purposed vegetables and fruits to nurture and strengthen our bodies. We should allow the Holy Spirit to lead us correctly in our eating habits. He will also motivate us to exercise our bodies.

We must pray for God's deliverance, healing, and strength to aid us in building our temple to be worthy of His Holy Spirit. The choices we make for our temples will either grieve the Holy Spirit or strengthen Him in us.

Strength in the Resting Place

How do we find strength in the resting place? There are times when we need encouragement in our lives to continue to press forward, remain faithful, and stay standing in God.

The only way we will find serenity and strength in our purpose is when we remain faithful to God.

God's resting place provided the strength needed in past times. There was a time when the families of David's army had been captured and taken away. Scripture tells us that, "*David and the people who were with him lifted their voices and wept until there was no strength in them to weep.*" (1 Samuel 30:4). And, all his men were furiously upset with David. It goes on to say that, "*David was greatly distressed because the men were considering stoning him; each one of them were cold in spirit because of his sons and daughters. But David found strength in the Lord God.*" (1 Samuel 30:6).

God will provide strength when we rest in His presence. We can do nothing through the natural means (self) without failure. We must continue to take time to meditate in God's Word, to love Him, and let Him love us. By the grace of God, we become strong in times of weariness. Grace is given to those who live and endure.

God rested on the seventh day. He completed all His creative work (see Genesis chapter 2) so he rested. God couldn't cease from righteousness because he is righteous. He couldn't cease from holiness because he is holy. God did not need to rest as He did not get weary. God never faints, neither is He weary. (Isaiah 40:28). God modeled rest so that we can follow.

Many people do not interpret the meaning of spiritual rest correctly. Spiritual rest doesn't mean that we are to cease from praying or ministering to others. When we take vacation, we cease from our day-to-day labor such as cooking, laundry, etc.). Though we may physically rest on vacation and leave our daily tasks behind for a few days, we remain obliged to take care of God's business wherever we go. Our responsibility to pray for the brokenhearted or feed a hungry soul never ceases.

As we enter into spiritual rest, we must position ourselves to worship and praise. We must begin to trust and believe that God will work on our behalf. Although there are times when God doesn't seem as if He is nearby, we must remain calm and faithful trusting His word. If He said it, believe it and we shall receive it!

Chapter 2

Commitment: A Consecrated Life

"Our people must learn to devote themselves to doing what is good, so they may provide for daily needs and not live unproductive lives."

(Titus 3:14 NIV)

Consecration means: anointing, blessing, canonization, dedication, devotion, exaltation, glorification, hallowing, making holy, ordination. We must prepare our hearts to orchestrate an uncompromising devotion to God.

Our attitudes and our actions must be in devotion to God. We cannot do "good" in our own will but only through the power of Christ who lives in us. Therefore, we must allow Christ to shape us; shape our attitude, thoughts, emotions, conversation, environment, and social network. We must turn over our will to God so our fidelity can lead us to the practices of what is good and acceptable for the Kingdom of God.

God will teach us to be productive once we commit to doing what is right in His eyes. Some believers feel obliged to live a life of Christianity by attending church services, joining a choir, and accepting the faith of salvation but fail to commit to it. Their attitudes lack commitment, desire, compassion, love, and sincerity. All these lead to empty devotion and unproductive lives. In this time of consecration, we must give our lives to God and allow the indwelling of the Holy Spirit to drive us to the road of victory and truth.

As consecration become habitual in our lives, holiness fills us thoroughly and brings us into personal communion with God. We need growing faith to have an enriching consecrated life. It takes prayer to preserve such an intimacy with God. Without persistent prayer, holiness will be interrupted. Consecration leaves us in a restorative place with God so that He can work His purpose in us.

Living in Consecration

Living in consecration undertakes a deeper level of spiritual purification. It brings us to humility and develops character. A consecrated life produces Christ-like qualities which include the fruit of the Spirit. It is the character of Christ that develops into a spiritual maturity that allows us to overcome weary circumstances and spiritual attacks during our walk with God.

Consecration occurs before purification begins. Consecration begins when the believer separates himself or herself from worldly affairs, such as drugs, alcohol, gambling, promiscuity (orgies, pornography). God is not going to take us away from the situation or take us out of the bed of affliction if we are reluctant to remove ourselves from impure acts (see Leviticus 20:7). We must practice what the Word of God says instead of submitting to the lethal reasoning of a corrupt mind. Consecration involves absolute surrender to God.

We want to stress that believers must withdraw from the detrimental acts that will condemn our souls. Greed, selfishness, lying, stealing, and adultery are some of the many parts of our sinful nature that will draw us away from God. When we turn away from sinful ways and habits, God will meet us at the cross and cleanse us by His Spirit. It is then we become accustomed to God's voice, and our lives will be surrendered to true worship and prayer.

When we are fully surrendered to God, thoughts, discussion, attire, appearance, diet, and relationships will be governed by the leading of the Holy Spirit.

Fasting and Praying

Believers can attain discipline, joy, faith and inner strength within their spiritual life by obedience and dedication. God's holiness is accessible if we just keep our heart and mind focused on Him.

Jehovah Jireh (God our provider) understands what His people need to live a life of consecration. As any loving parent would do to prepare their child for providing daily bread, God offers instructions on how and when to move.

One of the tools used in consecration is fasting. Oftentimes, the body of Christ is not disciplined enough to give up food when God asks them to interrupt their daily routine by doing so.

Fasting brings about change within the believer and it prepares us to hear from God. It increases the need for the heart to receive spiritual feeding and decrease the body's need of food.

Many of us take part in fasting for the wrong reason; to gain blessings. Fasting is not intended as a tool to lose weight, to change God's mind or to make an exchange of sacrifice. It is to move into the supernatural realm of power, authority and faith by denying the desires of flesh. When we are fasting, we need to hear from God, not friends, co-workers, relatives or even the pastor. Fasting is essential to clearly hear the voice of God. Without fasting, our spiritual mind-set can become so easily distracted.

Another tool used in consecration is prayer. During time in consecration, God requires us to give our ear to His voice, which means we must spend quality time in prayer. Today, many Christians pour out to God in prayer but do not allow God to pour in to them. Prayer is a two-way communication between God and the person praying. The exchange strengthens our faith and provides us with keys to open the door to God's power and authority.

Fasting and praying is the utmost spiritual discipline that brings us closer to God, giving Him room for divine intervention. The dual weapon of fasting and praying was used by the early Church as part of spiritual warfare (read Acts 14:23).

Matthew 16:19 tells us that God has given us the keys to the Kingdom of Heaven. The Church should utilize more often the keys of binding and loosing so there would not be so many defeats. We hear so many Christians owning sicknesses, diseases, failing relationships and financial bondage instead of exercising their power and authority of binding and loosing. As Christians, we are to grasp and use every key that Jesus has given us access to because we are to operate on earth as God does in heaven.

Overcoming Obstacles

There are many challenges and trials we must face in overcoming obstacles during consecration. Although consecration opens doors to spiritual blessings, there will be impediments of doubt, fear, loneliness and discouragement that will try to hinder us. We may struggle with surrendering our carnal thoughts, bad habits, past actions that were detrimental to us or others, and even an event that keeps us holding on to painful memories. However, we must resist temptation to reverting back to thoughts or emotions that will dismantle our commitment to God. If we pray for the Holy Spirit to help us with this, He will.

When we look at the life of King David, he faced and had to overcome many difficulties. Though the journey was painful, lonely and discouraging, David's life was disciplined in servant-hood for God's glory. David yielded his heart to serve the Lord because he made up his mind to do so.

As we experience feelings of defeat and emotional affliction, we can rest in the knowledge that God has the power to strengthen us in that terrible condition. During hard times, David embraced two positions: submission and commitment to the will of God. With grace and mercy, the spirit of God empowered David's life. He can and will do the same for us if we ask Him to.

Submission to God's Will

The term "*submission*" comes from the Greek word "*hupotasso*" which means to place under, subject to and obey (*Strong's #5293*). The power of submission lies within the heart and attitude of a righteous man. When we love someone, whether it is a spouse or a pastor, we are cooperative in yielding to his or her authority (Ephesians 5:21-33).

God doesn't force us to agree to His will. We have to make a choice to serve Him with all of our heart, mind and soul. When we submit to the will of God, we agree to give the Holy Spirit permission to help us overcome our struggles and remain obedient to God. We are placed under His authority to lead us in our weakness. During submission to God, He strengthens us to carry out our purpose and His will.

We are to worship God in holiness. This means we are to separate ourselves from every bad thought, emotion, and worldly nature when we are in the presence of the Lord. We can't do this through self-will; rather, we need the grace of God to lead us towards His will. God can only give us holy desires to stay disciplined, faithful in worship, and obey Him.

Commitment to God

Commitment to God leads us into a place of unfamiliarity or the unknown. We must trust in the Lord and develop an understanding of His Sovereignty. The depths of our intimacy with God will determine our love for God. Our love for God will determine our commitment to God.

Commitment to God will lead us into a possible wilderness. When God called Abraham to leave his father's house, kindred, and country, he did not know what was ahead of him (Genesis 12:1). Abraham lost control of his possessions, lost his relationship with his nephew Lot, and lost his level of comfort (Genesis 14:12). Despite his obstacles, Abraham committed to God and he ultimately received generational blessings (Hebrews 6:13-15). Our submission and commitment to God will aide us in overcoming our obstacles.

The Sovereignty of God

God is our main support during consecration. He is the one who gives us grace, mercy, compassion and strength. When we understand who our Creator is and what He can do, then we will no longer need to commit to fear, confusion, defeat and unrighteous living.

The preeminence of God stands alone. Since there is no greater, He can swear by Himself. He is the same God who split the Red Sea and later on dethroned Himself from heaven just to die on the Cross for you and me. It was God who created the earth in six days. It was God who resurrected Christ on the third day, whom imparted life to mankind. We can all agree that, *"For of Him, and through Him, and to Him are all things: to whom be glory forever. Amen."* (Romans 11:36).

We have to learn how to defeat opposition by speaking the Word of God and, like David did, encourage ourselves! We mustn't look at the things we don't have, but rather we must look at the things we do have. We have the Father,

Son, and Holy Spirit to support us through this period of consecration. It is the moment of truth when everything we possess is surrendered to God for His supreme use!

While in consecration, the sovereignty of God reveals to us a new insight of reverence for the influence and power of God. His sovereignty teaches us to embrace new insight into the order of His creation and divinity. We cannot live a full life without it. The power of God reveals a new paradigm shift away from our old thinking. God devised our thoughts without our minds conforming to the wickedness of the world. He designed our lives to be powered by the Holy Spirit until He returns for us.

We have free will and the Sovereignty of God is available to us. However, we cannot waste another hour procrastinating or contending with a holy God. Evil lurks in all four corners of the earth waiting for us to reject the power of God. We must strengthen our spiritual life and advance in spiritual maturity. Submit to the sovereignty of God, read his Word and seek Him daily until His rhema (spoken word) is revealed to you.

Chapter 3

The Union: Love & Holiness

"Love is patient, love is kind. It does not envy, it does not boast, it is not proud. It is not rude, it is not self-seeking, it is not easily angered, it keeps no record of wrongs. Love does not delight in evil but rejoices with the truth. It always protects, always trusts, always hopes, always perseveres. Love never fails..."
(1 Corinthians 13:4-8 NIV)

Holiness and love are interchangeable; one compliments the other. Holiness and love consummate an intimate union between the Holy Trinity (Father, Son and Holy Spirit) and the Church (called out ones). The power of this holy love and holiness is a demonstration of unity that draws others to Christ Jesus.

In order to perfect this union, Christians must be holy and walk in love as Christ has loved us. As we evangelize, we are called to love on a higher plane. Spiritual leaders in the church should use proper training to help their congregations understand how to effectively minister in love to the communities where they serve. There are people who are broken, hurt and in pain that need this special love.

Love is a powerful tool given to us by the Father to heal, deliver, protect, build relationships, discipline and correct. Believers are given the power to love others faithfully and consistently. *"Above all, love each other deeply, because love covers over a multitude of sins."* (1 Peter 4:8)

Surprisingly, many Christians do not understand the true meaning of love and how to demonstrate it; it's not just having compassion for humanity or having a loving relationship with a man or woman. It is simply giving oneself unconditionally to others.

Love is an unprejudiced and unconditional act that demonstrates care, correction and concern. This Godly love shows through with a clear distinction between a Christian and an unbeliever. Christians are recognized by the love shared with one another. If we do not love others, especially unbelievers, God's love is not in us.

Jesus said, *"I have not come to call the righteous but sinners to repentance."*(Luke 5:32) A doctor doesn't heal healthy people and healthy people do not seek treatment. Our responsibility is to particularly love those in need without reason and condition. Sadly, in our world, there are people who have never been loved. Bitterness and anger become their manifestation of this lack of love and it is the only way they know how to respond to the world. They are judged because no one understands that they are conformed to their hurts and pains. What they need is for someone to love them the way Christ loved.

Agape Love

Agape is the Greek name for love (*Strong's #26*). Jude 1:21 states, "Keep yourselves in the love of God." This type of love brings eternal reward to a believer's life on earth. *Agape* is God-centered love. It is a love that heals and saves. *Agape* love reaches out, forgives, and deals with people in need. When we walk in holiness, we cannot remain in this state without service to others in *Agape* love. There is a clear distinction between God-centered love (*Agape*) and earthly love (idols, lust, selfishness). *Agape* shows itself with a pure and sincere heart that draws others toward it. This love is a perfect and holy love.

Look at the personality of *Agape* love, "... *patient, kind, does not envy*" (1 Corinthians 13:4) If the body of Christ submits to this love, it will bring an abundance of healing and deliverance to all of us in need. A person who commits to *Agape* love as God directed, pours all of his or her body and soul into this service. One who exercises *Agape* love gives up, at no cost, his or her time, ability, money, ear to listen, shoulder to lean on, or whatever else is needed to assist in any situation. He or she understands the quality, price and heavenly reward of their submission.

A believer who shares *Agape* love brings loyalty, respect, and kindness and moves God's purpose forward. *Agape* love validates our relationship with Jesus. It expresses our Christian love towards God. Jesus says, "*Thou shalt love the Lord thy God with all thy heart, and with all thy soul, and with all thy mind.*" (read Matthew 22:36-38).

To be true believers and flowers we ought to have *Agape* love functioning and ruling in our hearts so we can love others the way God loves us. Christians should demonstrate love to all people, including those who live a lifestyle opposite of God's truth. Our *Agape* love brings hope to individuals who live unholy lifestyles. There may be a family or a church member who is struggling with a sinful lifestyle. It is imperative that we love them unconditionally. A scornful response to a fallen world brings more chaos and hatred.

However, when we teach, train and correct in love, the trespasser will be restored in righteousness and repent (Proverbs 9:8-9, Luke 17:3). When we love the sinners surrounding us, it distinctly demonstrates we want greater things for them; such as deliverance, healing and salvation.

This does not mean Christians accept unrighteous lifestyles. Though God hates sin, He doesn't hate the sinner. God is so merciful. The Bible states [inferences are ours], "...*for he* (God) *maketh his sun to rise on the evil* (lifestyles or acts deviated from the Word of God) *and on the good* (righteous lifestyle the way God views it), *and sendeth rain on the just* (righteous, those who are in right standing before God) *and on the unjust* (not right standing before God)." (Matthew 5:45b).

God is a fair and loving God who loved us first before we loved Him. If God had not loved us while we were his enemies, we could have never become His heirs. God commits Himself to love everyone no matter if the person is a Christian or a murderer. If He didn't love us as sinners, then the human race would never be given an opportunity to receive Jesus as Lord and Savior. *Through God's agape love, sinners will be drawn to salvation by divine appointment.*

Eros Love

Eros was a Greek and Roman god of love. (The American Heritage® Abbreviations Dictionary, Third Edition). He was the son of Aphrodite. He is better known by his Roman name Cupid. The Greek name is known for passionate or romantic love. *Eros* love is an emotional and physical attraction. It is a mixture of emotions such as anger, sexual urge, happiness, jealousy. It brings forth an intense delight for a moment of temporary passion. Paul says, *"For it is better to marry than to burn with passion."* (1 Corinthians 7:9b NIV). In other words, Paul was saying not to burn with the harmful flame of lust that comes from *Eros* because it will ruin the soul of man. He was saying that we can escape the lust by committing to one person through marriage.

Lust is a sin and the wages of sin is death (Romans 6:23a). So if our heart sins without repentance, then our whole being (spirit, body, soul) will be condemned to eternal death. Many Christians yield to the spirit of lust. They build their marriages on it, but it doesn't last. The fiery passion of sexual and romantic interaction should not rule in a marriage because once it goes out, the marriage ceases to be a marriage.

Some people ignorantly accept that not being in-love with their spouse is an excuse for walking out of the marriage! *Eros* is a benefit in a marriage, not the qualification for a marriage.

In terms of relationships, many people today pursue relations with intentions that are false, irrelevant, and last only a short time. They choose their partner based on their attraction for the other person or based on the other person's appearance, instead of seeking God's purpose and the genuine heart of the other person. The Bible states that "*for the LORD seeth not as man seeth; for man looketh on the outward appearance, but the LORD looketh on the heart*" (1 Samuel 16:7).

As Christians, we are called to pursue the spiritual things of God, which are eternal. We need to be mindful of how we use *Eros* in our relationships, especially ones that are new. We do not want the foundation of our relationships to be built primarily on *Eros* because the foundation would be provisional and not purposeful.

Phileo Love

Phileo is a Greek word "to treat affectionately or kindly, to welcome, befriend" (*Strong's #5368*). This love includes emotional warmth and tender affection toward friends, family members, and not limited to strangers (read 1 Peter 1:22). It can be used when referring to companionship. *Phileo* love involves mutual sharing in brotherly way in a relationship, friendship, and non-sexual context.

One radical change in the new-birth stage is that it brings about love for the brother or sister in Christ. One of God's attributes is love. Because God loves us, it makes it easier to love Him and others. When we commit ourselves to God and His Word, it purifies our hearts and souls and frees us from false perceptions or negativity surrounding another person that will hinder us in loving them.

Because of our fallen nature, we are incapable of producing pure *Phileo* love without Jesus. If we are to love as God loves, that *Phileo* love can only come from its true source, God! God commanded us to love each other. We need to keep our hearts pure and filled with that attitude of love. When that love is in our hearts, we can obey Jesus who said, "*I give you a new commandment, that you love one another. As I have loved you, you should also love one another.*" (John 13:34). This new commandment entails loving each other as He loved us, sacrificially, even to the point of death.

God's Demonstration of His Love

Let us take a further look to see how God demonstrated His love. Israel was a small and unknown tribe of people chosen by God. They were not better than any of the other tribes, but "*God hath chosen the foolish things of the world, to confound the wise: and God hath chosen the weak things of the world, to confound the things which are mighty*" (1 Corinthians 1:27). God's ultimate purpose for Israel was to produce the Messiah from the line of Abraham, Isaac, Jacob, and David. In addition, God wanted to use Israel to evangelize the world, to expand the kingdom of God, and point others towards the light.

Israel continued to sin against God. But God knew their shortcomings and downfalls. Instead of imposing judgment on them, God graciously sent the Messiah to free them from their sins. The Messiah was rejected by Israel, so he extended the gospel to the gentiles through his disciples. The Messiah became a two-fold blessing, one to Israel and the other was for the Gentiles. God called us all out of our sinful nature and into His holiness so we might not only be saved from His eternal judgment but that we can glorify Him on earth. That's love!

In essence, *Eros* love is "physical", *Phileo* love is "caring or affectionate brotherly love", and *Agape* love is spiritual and "holy" love. True love is tested and it will remain forever. Christians must always operate in a love that will accommodate God's purpose and draw unbelievers back to God. Let us aim for holiness in love.

Chapter 4

Living with Holiness

"As obedient children, not fashioning yourselves according to the former lusts in your ignorance: But as he which hath called you is holy, so be ye holy in all manner of conversation; Because it is written, Be ye holy; for I am holy."

(1 Peter 1:14-16)

A Church without holiness leaves preaching, teaching, and lifestyles voided. We must stay committed to holiness and walk in holiness as an example of how to live.

If we are filled with unholy thoughts and attitudes, then we cannot give God the reverence He is due. If we behave this way, we lose our power to influence the world on His behalf. A believer cannot remain blameless unless he or she is under the power of Jesus' blood. God's promise to us is to save us from sins through grace and to keep us through His holiness.

God wants us to be holy in every area of our lives. Holiness is a requisite for righteous living and a discipline for believers. It must be made perfect (mature) in us so we can stand before a holy God and live a peaceful life. Hebrews 12:14, declares, *"Follow peace with all men, and holiness, without which no man shall see the Lord."*

To see God means to enjoy His fellowship and presence on earth and to spend eternity with Him. God intended for us to be holy because He knew that holiness was the only way to be pure in heart, pure in conscience, and pure in our natural body. God wants us to keep our hearts and souls right so we can continue to enjoy His fellowship. When our hearts and souls are in the right place with God, we will joyfully and cheerfully obey biblical standards out of a heart of love and peace. With love and peace in our hearts we keep His commandments close and will witness to those in need of healing and deliverance.

Compromising Holiness

Some churches opened their doors to false teaching. They are filled with a lack of correction and lack of respect for God. They have backslidden. Believers must recognize that backsliding compromises holiness, our relationship with God and our obedience to Him.

God has commissioned His people to live kingdom principles governed by biblical standards. For example, one of the biblical standards are; *"Thou shalt not commit adultery. ...whosoever looketh on a woman to lust after her hath committed adultery with her already in his heart."* (Matthew 5:27-28) We cannot preach to others that infidelity is wrong while we lust after someone else' spouse. Some believers deem that God's standards are too high. They feel they can please God on their own by being "super-religious" and they create their own standard of righteousness.

Self-righteousness is a stubborn and prideful spirit. It hinders believers from attaining a joyful and peaceful life. It limits a person's ability to seek the truth in Christ. Those who are affected by the spirits of self-righteousness, pride, stubbornness and worldly compromise cannot discern unrighteousness from righteousness. They are to repent and seek God's guidance and correction.

Compromising to worldly standards will make us more vulnerable, ineffective and a complacent group of people open to sinfulness. Because of the compromises some fellowships make, the world often views the Church as hypocrites with false pretenses about its religion, beliefs, and relationship with God. When we compromise to worldly standards, it destroys the true image that God intends for His church. However, if we lead others by uncompromising in our fellowships, God is able to reverse false and destructive perceptions against the church by proving who He really is through us as an example.

Without holiness, the church loses its passion to draw others to God. Preaching about cars, homes and money doesn't glorify God. It only draw our desire to serve materialistic items instead of focusing on intangible values for the kingdom of God. We cannot serve two masters! If we are going to be righteous then be righteous and live that way! We must not and cannot be fence sitters. It is very important to remember that our choices will affect others around us. They affect our children, spouses, friends, and those who are around us watching how we behave.

Life of Obedience

Obedience plays a major part in all areas of Christianity. (In chapter five, we will discuss obedience to the cross.) Obedience is the outward expression of salvation. Holiness requires our obedience.

Whenever there is a lack of obedience in our character, holiness becomes obscured in our life. Obedience sustains our holiness. Obedience is not for us to think on, but to do; according to what is written in His Word. Act on the Word of God. The spirit of obedience is the precursor to holiness ruling in our lifestyles, ministries, and relationships. Obedience will guard us from the "*old man*" of our past, rising into our present, and affecting the future.

Our daily conduct should not model the world's behavior. The way we conduct ourselves in the world is evidence of whose we belong to. For example, "*The wicked borroweth, and payeth not again: but the righteous sheweth mercy, and giveth.*" (Psalms 37:21). The blessings of God are so high for the believer that we are able to show mercy and give to others.

God is not commanding us to be holy because of our position in the church or to be holy because it seems like the right choice. God declared us holy when we first accepted Jesus as our Lord and Savior (through salvation). He wants us to recognize why we are holy. We are holy because we serve a holy God who is pure in holiness, glorious in holiness, and is the source of holiness in others. We cannot operate in ministry without holiness. We cannot set an example for others without holiness. The world should witness our holiness not only in church, but during our interactions at our jobs, in the grocery store, on the highway or at the doctor's office.

The Spirit of Excellence

God has already placed us under His wing of righteousness, so all we need do is raise our level of consciousness and excellence. One way to do this is by expanding our knowledge through reading the Word of God daily. Raising our level of excellence means to humble ourselves and follow the leading of the Holy Spirit. He will guide us through every step if we follow with faith. The spirit of excellence is the attitude and characteristic of the Holy Ghost. It is the image of God. An example of how the spirit of excellence operates in the life of a believer can be found in *Daniel 1:20*. In every difficult situation, Daniel, Hananiah, Mishael, and Azariah came out 10 times better. By our faith in Christ Jesus, our hearts are regenerated with the spirit of excellence. Just as Daniel and the Hebrew boys did, God expects us to continue in excellence. It is the spirit of excellence that will bring stability in our walk with God, peace, joy, love and power to the body of Christ.

We too can hold the keys to excellence when we submit to holiness. These keys will drive the influences of the devil out of our places of worship. It will destroy every stronghold in our lives. We should make excellence a habit and exercise it daily within the Church. If we are not applying ourselves in every manner with the spirit of excellence, then how can we expect God to flow in our ministry, marriage and daily tasks? If we want more of God's glory in our lives, we must live with excellence as our goal.

God has not created anything without excellence and He doesn't expect us to perform at a level below excellence. The spirit of excellence will bring unity so there isn't any strife or division in our work. There is only one body, one mind and one spirit. Unity brings excellence. Excellence will aid us in fulfilling every potential that God has already placed within us.

Without excellence in our lives, we can easily continue in self-righteousness. David followed his own righteousness during his reign as King of Israel and Judah. Out of all his sins, perhaps adultery with Bathsheba (2 Samuel 12) was the most errant because he could have lost his passion and purpose for God. His unfaithfulness was a monumental sin, and then a subsequent sin (murder) was added to cover the first sin (adultery). God offered him grace to come clean and mend his ways, but David continued his intimacy with Bathsheba. So God sent the prophet Nathan to rebuke him.

Finally, David repented and God exacted His judgment on him. After having his first child with Bathsheba, the child was struck with sickness. David began to fast and consecrate himself to holiness. Although, his son died as a result of the sin, David still remained king and continued in His purpose.

Many Christians become so entangled with the world's practices that they fail to keep God's commands. This leads them to follow their own ways and standards which is in conflict with God's path. At first, they start off on the right path with God, but they somehow forget about the One who blessed them and allow self-righteousness to overtake them. When this happens, the ways of the world take over and many fall into self-righteous habits. God wants us to live in holiness and live accordingly or else we can lose our most valuable gift—salvation.

Keeping Faith in Holiness

True holiness is the result of our faith. It is impossible to persevere in faith without holiness. When we place our faith in Christ, the righteousness of Christ is upon us. That is the reason we can freely receive baptism in the Holy Spirit. We are vulnerable when we don't pursue and practice true holiness. Our faith will lead us out of our sinful nature.

Our faith helps us realize that our sins must change to righteous living before we are destroyed. If we continue in a sinful corrupted condition, relying on our own efforts or abilities, we cannot take part in fellowship with Christ.

A backslider relies on his or her own abilities instead of keeping faith in Christ. When we affirm our faith in Christ, it covers us with the righteousness of God. When we rely on our own strength to make things right with God, we fall into pride which leads to an inevitable and fall. We are to have genuine faith in Christ. This genuine working faith covers us and our works with God's righteousness.

Without holiness, there is no accountability in one's action. Christian leaders must display integrity, honesty, and be as blameless as is humanly possible. All believers must prove accountability in our works; however, spiritual leaders are the forefront of ministry, so God requires more of them.

The negative effect on the Church increases rapidly when Christian leaders fall short of God's glory. These failures challenge the confidence in spiritual leadership. Imprudent behavior minimizes the influence of the church as an honorable authority. The loss of holiness is not due only to the lack of biblical teachings or leadership incompetence. It stems from the fallen state of mind that weakens faith; beliefs that go beyond the modern day disorders of corruption and promiscuity.

If those who have fallen repent to God and embrace His holiness, then God will help them live a clean life that sets an example for the Church. Holiness is not a skill, talent, rank, title or position. It is a divine discipline that results in Christ-like quality.

Without holiness, there is no transformation in our lives. Christ, who is the living Word, is the source of our transformation into the image of God, *"And we all...beholding the glory of the Lord, are being transformed into the same image from one degree of glory to another."* (2 Corinthians 3:18, ESV2). God transforms us to reflect the fullness of His character.

Transformation begins with grace but it continues through spiritual discipline. Christians must pursue holiness by studying the Word of God. The more we study, the more Christ-like we become. The more we become like Christ, the more we win others to Him.

Holiness in Conversation

God has called us to be holy in our conversations to keep us from becoming a reproach to the gospel of Jesus Christ. Our words are the source of our testimony before the world. We've witness church folks coarsely joking in a way that is so offensive to others. This behavior is unacceptable to God. Our conversations should not include gossip. Every discussion we engage in should be clean and pure. We shouldn't be entertained with coarse joking or derogatory conversations, *"Nor should there be obscenity, foolish talk or coarse joking, which are out of place, but rather thanksgiving"* (Ephesians 5:4 NIV).

Holiness should lead our conversation with thanksgiving and praise to God. Our conversation should not include things that are not in the will of God. God intends for us to be healed, so if one needs healing, speak words of healing. If we need a financial breakthrough, speak words of prosperity. We should never speak words of defeat, no matter what our circumstances look or feel like.

In our stand for Christ, we will face adversities and stumbling blocks, but we can begin to declare what God has said in His Word. There is nothing too hard for the Lord. If we need something, we are to say something! God told Abraham to ask for all the land which he saw. God promised that He would give it to Abraham and his seed (Genesis 13:14-15). Abraham had to speak those "things" that were not, as though they were.

We have so much power in our words. With positive words we can encourage our children, spouse, friends, co-worker and those we come in contact with. With negative words, we can tear down a heart because *"Life and death are in the power of the tongue."* (Proverbs 18:21 ESV).

Chapter 5

The Virtue of Patience

"My brethren, count it all joy when ye fall into divers temptations; Knowing this, that the trying of your faith worketh patience. But let patience have her perfect work, that ye may be perfect and entire, wanting nothing."

(James 1:2-4)

One of the provisions of Christ is to bear and to bring forth the fruit of the Spirit. God expects for us to bear patience as part of our cross. When we endure trials and tribulations, God uses it as an opportunity to perfect his purpose in us.

Change is inevitable because it prepares us to grow, whether it is in ministry, relationships or work. We have no control or influence over when these things will take place. However, there are things that we must work on within ourselves in order to be prepared for change God proposes for our lives. If we wait with increasing anxiety instead of hope, then our faith is rooted in the wrong place.

Patience should be demonstrated during trials. Patience exposes the truth about faith in God's eternity for us. Patience does not come overnight. We can't throw a cake mix into the oven for ten minutes and expect a mouthwatering dessert as the end result. While the cake (your character) is baking, rejoice in the Lord with gratitude!

How do we wait on God to heal us when our bodies are inflicted with pain? How do we wait on God to provide us with a financial breakthrough? How do we wait on God to change a particular matter in a marriage without losing hope? We wait in joyful patience and faith!

Endure With Patience

Endurance produces character. Through hard labor and suffering, God teaches us to be disciplined even while we wait on Him to show us the direction He wants us to take. This means, if God has called us to serve in a particular ministry or work at a specific place, then He expects for us to stay there until He moves us out of that place. If we do not wait on Him and endure, we might be at risk of forfeiting someone else's blessing or even our own.

In our Christian living, we are expected to maintain self-control and to be rooted in the Word of God. Surrendering to Him can be a painful process of endurance and waiting as we learn the lessons we need to learn. During the waiting period we must make the point of setting aside time and finding a quiet place to allow God to give us direction. This quiet time is a time to repent, rebuke any sinful distraction and recommit our relationship to God.

As we wait on the Lord, it is critical to refresh and restore our minds with divine equity and authority through Christ Jesus. We cannot allow ourselves to succumb to irrational reasoning or self- gratifying thoughts. At times, we may feel defeated or experience feelings of worthlessness because it doesn't feel good waiting on situations to change. However, God is not going to lead us out of our situation because it doesn't 'feel good'. He is calling us to endure in our journey until we are able to see outside ourselves and think outside ourselves. We can't quit! We must ask God to fill our hearts and minds with peace and plant our feet on the path of righteousness for His glory.

Abiding in Patience

Patience must abide in all believers for greater growth in our relationships, ministries and in our purpose. The Greek word for abide is Meno (*Strong's# 3306*). Meno means "*to remain, abide*". There is no inference for precisely how long we must dwell in that place God wants us to be in; however, waiting on God means embracing His will until He tells us to move.

Patience provides tolerance as we wait for something to change, as we endure trials and overcome battles. It may be an uncomfortable experience, but we must not move! We may not like the environment of our waiting season, but we should not try to reason in our own understanding. We must embrace our situation and rest in it. Acting upon our feelings is not an option. Acting in our natural senses (taste, feel, smell, hear and see) can forfeit us out of the perfect will of God. We must not let our natural senses cut us loose from God's flow of moving us into our strategic positions.

Patience in God shifts our confidence in Him from rocky to firm! The art of patience makes sanctification evident, bringing about a profound joy, a peaceful heart and a total oneness with the Lord. Even so, waiting with patience develops character and spiritual maturity. A believer who is not spiritually mature in his/her walk will struggle in the waiting process. Our attitude exhibits our maturity or lack thereof in our faith and actions. A person who stagnates in his or her faith is not stable; for example, yesterday we plead the blood of Jesus, believing in the Word of God and expecting a financial breakthrough any minute; and today, we are moved by emotions and begin to panic because the bill collectors call on the job.

A spiritually mature believer will pray during adversity, guard his or her tongue from evil, and seek to make peace even in conflict. Spiritual maturity has nothing to do with a person's age. It has everything to do with character and attitude. It is easy to be in control and to display a pleasant attitude when everything is working out to our satisfaction. How do we handle unforeseen adversity? Are we filled with anger or lack self-control? God is calling His people to endure, have patience and continue to depend on Him to supply every need, according to His riches and glory in Christ Jesus (Philippians 4:9).

Being Obedient to the Voice of God

"Behold, to obey is better than sacrifice" (1 Samuel 15:22). Obedience is the conduit for believers to expand the kingdom of God; we are to be used as a vessel for service..

Obedience teaches us to be disciplined and conscientious in our actions. It is not a pleasant experience to be corrected by God. However, it can help remove obstacles and stubbornness that can block our ears from hearing God. Without obedience, there is no sharing in God's holiness.

Our obedience and faithful response to the call of God will help us develop a righteous life of good works. We must commit and be obedient to God. Just as God's holiness brings Him glory, our obedience reaps holiness and allows us to reach out to others in need of His glory. As we follow the call of God, we will reap the blessings from God in our ministry.

The truth is available to us but we must prepare ourselves for rightful living through prayer, fasting and reading the Word daily. The time has come for us to realize that God demands total obedience. In total obedience, He can provide us with more insight, more discernment, more power, more wisdom, more strength and more love. Everything we do is for the glory of God. God did not bring us into disobedience and discontent; His plan is to bring salvation–through Christ– to every believer.

Preparation for Change

When change is about to occur, consecration (the solemn dedication to a special purpose or service) may be necessary to fulfill its purpose. Consecration is a process of preparing for change. It seeks to eliminate past habits and experiences that will hinder you from hearing God. Where there is consecration, there is also transformation.

To be transformed in our minds requires us to yield to God while in the process of changing. It may require us to give up something which could be painful, depending on how much we are willing to submit and how emotionally attached we are to the object needing to be surrendered. For example, you are expecting a promotion on the job when God is trying to make you an entrepreneur. He prepares us in such a way, that it won't break our focus or hinder our thoughts.

People embrace change more readily when it happens gradually rather than when it occurs quickly. Normally, without life threatening illnesses, accidental or intentional injuries, we are supposed to grow old gracefully. Our bodies begin to break down gradually, wrinkles begin to creep in gradually and gross motor skills begin to slow down. On the other hand however, the sudden loss of a spouse forces us to shift our position without preparation. If we do not yield to God's will, change can become a torment. It is best to let God perform His spiritual work in us; yielding to the peace of God and continuing to follow His plan for our lives. We must not turn back and give up on our walk in salvation. God is working on us so we must be still and embrace the beauty of His presence.

Understanding Humility

Humility brings us closer to Christ and self-centeredness gets thrown out of the equation. Devoting ourselves to humility brings calmness to our spirits. Let me be the first to say that it is not easy to stand in humility when you have to deal with opposition at work or remain silent when someone is accusing you viciously. Humility displays a Christ-like attitude towards a spiritual life. Therefore, believers must practice responding to others in meekness.

There are many examples that Christ used to demonstrate humility. One example was when Jesus washed the feet of his disciples. Another example was when Christ died on the Cross. Humility does not mean that we are cowards. It does not mean that we should allow other people to assassinate our character. It simply means that we should have respect towards God and deny ourselves. We must put other people's needs before our own. We must forgive when we really don't want to. We must love someone even when they can't stand to be in the same room with us or wishing us harm. Humility is difficult but it is not impossible.

We become perfect in humility when there is a deadness to self that shows God and men a true transformation of self. To master anything requires us to practice it consistently. Although humility brings power to the inner self, it is hardly ever desirous from a human perspective because it can be painful to give up pride and high opinion of ourselves.

God may keep us humble by placing a permanent thorn in our flesh (2 Corinthians 7:12). When we yield to the righteousness of God, we will find a place of humility. If we remain there we will be blessed, receive power and attain joy. The deeper our pleasure in humility, the greater advance we make in holiness.

Chapter 6

Authority Over the Works of the Flesh

"Now the works of the flesh are manifest,...Adultery, fornication, uncleanness, lasciviousness, idolatry, witchcraft, hatred, variance, emulations, wrath, strife, seditions, heresies, envyings, murders, drunkenness, revellings, and such like... they which do such things shall not inherit the kingdom of God."
(Galatians 5:19-21)

Many of our decisions come from lack of knowledge or from being emotionally driven. There are constant spiritual battles in the lives of believers. The flesh is also one of the greatest obstacles in the life of the believer. The works of the flesh are characteristics of the sinful nature of man caused by sinful desires.

The manifestation of the works of the flesh is always in opposition of the fruit of the Spirit in the life of every believer. The flesh hinders the flow of holiness in our lives. It is our advantageous to use the authority that Jesus delegated to us to block Satan's attempt to hinder righteous living.

Wherever the authority of Jesus is called upon, it breaks through the chaos and undisciplined behavior.

When we are under His appointed authority, we have a valid and authoritative source to draw from. We must be held accountable when we are given this authority. For example, a deacon is accountable for his duties to his pastor (or overseer), a wife is accountable for her household to her husband, an employee is accountable for his or her work to his or her employer, and so forth. If we rebel against those in authority we are essentially rebelling against God: "*Let every soul be subject unto the higher powers. For there is no power but of God; the powers that be are ordained of God. Whosoever therefore resisteth the power, resisteth the ordinance of God: and they that resist shall receive to themselves damnation.*" (Romans 13:1-2)

The Bible says, "Be not conformed to this world." (Romans 12:1). When we conform to disorder, we subject ourselves to failing power and authority. In order for us to keep our power and authority over the works of the flesh, we must maintain a godly reverence, submission to God, and keep our lives in decency and order.

Godly Reverence

The church must stand against the traditions of worldly value and begin to revere God. If we want to take authority over our fleshly desires, then it is vital for us to walk in the ways of God. We must often remind ourselves that God has the ultimate choice and power to destroy all of us. He has the power to allow and disallow defeat and victory in our lives; as He wills. He is the creator of every living thing on earth. Yet, some people live their lives without fear of God.

Reverence is profound respect towards God. We ought to exalt, respect and be in awe of God in private and in public. There are times people behave inappropriately in church by gossiping with other members, chatting on cell phones while service is in progress, or when they bring food and coffee to church. That is a total disrespect to God! Instead of gossiping in church, we should be meditating on the Word of God, praying for others or tending to our Father's business. Once we begin to revere God, we can then honor sacred places and those who are in authority.

Reverence in a marriage sets proper tone, as the wife subjects to her husband and the husband to his wife. Although the husband is not superior in the marriage, wives must respect the biblical responsibility God created for man.

Home affects ministry and ministry is the greater responsibility. 1 Timothy 3:5 says, "For if a man know not how to rule his own house, how shall he take care of the church of God?" In home environments, children should not have the same authority as their parents. Decisions can be compromised by the parent when the child holds no reverence. If the home is not in order, then the proper leadership in ministry will not be exercised. Behavior should be consistent whether we are at home or in church.

There are several scriptures written in the Bible that parents can follow to work with their children in developing a reverential attitude (Proverbs 3:11-12, Exodus 20:12, Proverbs 13:24). When parents base their decisions on the Word of God and remain consistent in their discipline, children will become more conscientious with parental authority. They will begin to revere parents as they should. If believers stay consistent in applying rules at home that are based on the Word, it will also bring reverence and order back into the church.

There are moments when spiritual leaders do not address the sinful activities exhibited in churches. They've avoided correction (and disciplinary actions) of their members/ministers for living overpowering lifestyles of drunkenness, fornication, adultery and homosexuality according to the governance of biblical scripture. These behaviors can ultimately become so acceptable to the body of Christ, it will not be easily recognizable. When the leaders of the church do not respond properly and according to the Word to correct and discipline their members, other members are at risk of conforming to the patterns of worldly lifestyles. Reverence to God becomes secondary. However, when the sinner is addressed, privately or openly, it is the leading of the Holy Ghost that will convict spirits and discipline people back to Godly reverence. Leaders must be in compliance to the leading of the Holy Spirit.

Compliance through Submission

The Bible says to, "*Submit yourselves to every ordinance of man for the Lord's sake: whether it be to the king, as supreme; Or unto governors, as unto them that are sent by him for the punishment of evildoers, and for the praise of them that do well.*" (1 Peter 2:13-14-KJV). If we want to take authority over our fleshly desires, then we must learn how to submit to authority. Being in compliance means to be in agreement. The Holy Spirit doesn't force you to do anything. He only lead you to do the will of God. We can start by asking the Holy Spirit to assist us and then yield to His leading. We must submit ourselves one to another in the fear of God (Ephesians 5:21). This means that wives submit to husbands, husbands submit to God, children submit to parents, church members submit to the spiritual leaders, workers submit to supervisors and so forth. If we do not submit to God, then we open doors to evil thoughts and desires. *"For from within, out of the heart of men, proceed evil thoughts, fornications, thefts, murders, adulteries,"* (Mark 7:21). Not submitting to God will manifest our behavior to the submission of the works of the flesh. The works of the flesh is the outward manifestation of the desires within the heart and mind. A child of the Most High God should not entertain his or her thoughts with vain imaginations. God tells us to cast down imaginations and every high thing that exalt itself against the knowledge of God (2 Corinthians 10:5). If the mind drifts or remains focused on something unclean, then we ought to rebuke it without compromising our feelings, emotions and desires.

James says, *"Submit yourselves therefore to God. Resist the devil, and he will flee from you."* (James 4:7). Our power and authority lies in our submission to God. Joseph had the power to resist Potiphar's wife because of his submission to God's righteousness. He did not submit to his emotions. His flesh was willing but his soul was saying, *"What profit is it to a man if he gains the whole world, and loses his own soul? Or what will a man give in exchange for his soul?"* (Mark 8:36-37). Our souls are made for God. They can never integrate with the righteousness of God; neither will our souls have peace and happiness, until they are saved from sin.

Man is more spirit than he is flesh; but man allows the flesh to overshadow the spirit. Some of us will not take part in addressing the issues of sin in our lives or in other's lives because of fear, greed and lust (temporary satisfaction). One of the many reasons church leaders fail in correcting members is because either they fear losing members or that they've become too "familiar" with members. Familiarity hinders the power of authority and hinders a positive attitude of reverence towards the leader.

The Disciplinary of God

God humbles us through discipline. He may humble us by suffering, disappointment, loss, and sacrifice. These are all part of the Christian walk. If God doesn't correct us, then the spirit of pride will show up. When pride shows up, we look to "self" and not to God. Eventually, we fall!

There are also church members who do not want to adhere to correction. They do not want to hear the truth about their unclean behavior because of pride and rebellion. We cannot continue to live unclean lives and still preserve our salvation. Our lives need correction from God through spiritual leaders. God places leaders in positions of authority to keep us from falling. It is important that we align our lives with submission to God's Word to protect our souls from failing God's purpose. In 1 Peter 2:11, it states that we should "abstain from fleshly lusts, which war against the soul". If we protect our souls and minds, then we can begin to reign over the battles of the works of the (unclean) flesh.

Decency and Order

The scripture says, *"Let all things be done decently and in order."* (1 Corinthians 14:40). From the very beginning of the world, God created a structure to bring order out of confusion. He instituted structures of authority in every area of life. He created the Holy Trinity (God the Father, Jesus the Son, and the Holy Spirit). God saw it as a necessity to establish other structures of authority which affect our lives, for example, governments, husbands, parents, supervisors, pastors etc. These authorities aid us in keeping order in our lives.

If we want to take authority over our fleshly desires, then we must maintain decency and order in our lives that will keep us away from confusion and disorderly behaviors. This behavior separates us from God's holiness and purpose. For example, adultery destroys marriages. A marriage bed that has been defiled destroys the covenant of *"being one flesh."* (Genesis 2:24). Though the marriage can be reconciled by the power of repentance and forgiveness, it can affect others involved, such as children.

To keep decency in our lives means that we remain free from obscenity, rudeness, vulgarity, discourtesy and impoliteness. We should be honest and display kind behavior. By keeping our minds purified and filled with God's word, it stops the doors of the works of the flesh from opening.

God called all things to be in order. He called it in heaven first and then on earth. The dark came first so light could shine (see Genesis 1:2). When behaviors or the environment are out of order, it creates darkness and emptiness. It feels unpleasant and compromising to the spirit.

Christians have authority to control the environment by staying under the directions of the Holy Spirit. Psalm 37:23 says, "*The steps of a good man are ordered by the LORD: and he delighteth in his way.*" When our steps are ordered by God, there are no failures or discrepancies in our walk. There is pleasure, enjoyment, and peace no matter what we have to go through.

The Fruits of the Spirit

The Bible emphasizes, "*Wherefore by their fruits you shall know them*" (Matthew 7:20). God cares about the fruits we bear rather than the deeds of our own righteousness. Some people give the outward appearance of being a spiritual light, but inwardly they do not manifest divine fruits or the Christ-like character.

The fruits, or spiritual qualities shown by a person, will reveal who the person really is and who he or she serves. We must be aware of the deeds of self-righteousness. If we look at a person's life, it reveals his or her fruits and character. The fruit of the Spirit is love, joy, peace, longsuffering, gentleness, goodness, faith, meekness, and temperance. These are all Christ-like qualities.

Jude warned against those who have crept into the church and teach false doctrine (Jude vs. 4). He said one of the ways to recognize character is by the type of fruit (or figs) in their lives.

Galatians 5:22-23 lists the fruits of the Spirit. This divine fruit produces vitamins Cs: Character and Commitment. They bring maturity to the life of the believer. We may be experiencing the difficulties of living a holy life but we must continue to pursue fruits no matter what we go through. We must ask God to bring maturity to our character so we are able to handle the burdens in life. Whenever we fall short of His glory, we should confess and repent immediately so bad habits won't hinder our Christ-like character.

The people of God have become immersed in their sins and their character is now unrefined. Some of us have false motives that drive us away from our purpose. Despite these failures, God chose us to be set apart from the world. The only way out of these failures is to focus on Jesus' attributes and qualities. They will only develop in us as we continue to walk in the power of the Holy Spirit.

When a person lacks fruits, they have no self-control. People who have no self-control are compulsive in their ways, for example eating excessively, drinking alcohol or having temper tantrums. When we lack fruits, our spirit lets us know we need deliverance in an area in our life. If we ignore the need for deliverance, the doors to the works of the flesh open. When we look to fulfill our own desires, our sight will be blinded by truth as we become disobedient to God. To avoid falling into this pit, we need to do frequent self-examinations to make sure that we don't have habits and behaviors that aren't pleasing to God.

Some people have no concern or compassion for others. They pretend to bear the fruit of goodness by performing many deeds, yet their hearts are far from love. They pretend to bear the fruit of love by helping someone. They pretend that they want to serve until you ask them to do something humble such as mopping the church floors or ushering at a special service. True humility means accepting the short end of a stick even when the measurement of your deed is far expecting for a reward. A person with true humility does not pat themselves on the back or wait to receive brownie points from others.

If these believers do not get recognition for their deeds, they develop negative attitudes or withdraw. Some people want to be known by their deeds so that they "look good'. They will give gifts, spend time with others, and do whatever it takes to be acknowledged. But, if the attitude and the deed don't glorify God, it is not true fruits. Whenever God is glorified, a believer will express joy in good deeds even without recognition.

In ministries today, the people are focusing on the gifts (*Word of Wisdom, Word of Knowledge, Faith, Gifts of Healing, Working of Miracles, Prophecy, Discerning of Spirits, Divers* (or different) *kinds of Tongues, and Interpretation of* (different) *Tongues*-(see 1 Corinthians 12) rather than the fruits of the Holy Spirit. Jesus said that many would be deceived by the miracles wrought by the anti-Christ during the end times. He wasn't speaking of unbelievers, but believers. Many believers have allowed themselves to fall into deception and unconsciously follow deceiving spirits. But God is speaking to the Church today. If we do not bear fruits, He will raise up a nation who is willing to do so. (Matthew 21:43). God will always have a group of people prepared for His purpose.

Because of Israel's denial to bear fruit, God planned for a gentile nation to receive the gospel of the kingdom. From the gentiles, God raised up the Church to fulfill His plan of spiritual reproduction throughout the world. We must not allow the enemy to overpower us through the works of the flesh. We must walk in the Spirit of God every day. Paul said, "*Let no man deceive you by any means; for that day shall not come except there comes a falling away first,..*" (2 Thessalonians 2:3). Present yourself to God with pure motives and with readiness of mind. This will reinforce our authority in God.

Exercising Our Spiritual Fruits

It is a joy to see ministries demonstrating spiritual gifts; however, there is a lack of exercising spiritual fruits. We must exercise our spiritual fruits for them to be productive for the kingdom of God. If we are patient with one group of people in church, but lack patience at home with our children we cannot feel too satisfied. Every day we need to check our fruits and ask ourselves: Are we operating in love or anger? Are we kind to strangers and rude to those who are dear to our hearts?

The more fruits of the spirit we produce in our lives, the more mature we become in Christ. Just as human physical growth requires nutrition, spiritual growth requires food (Word of God), exercise (action of the Word of God), and time (meditation). All of the gifts we exercise should stream from love. As we operate in love, our spiritual fruits develop to full capacity. Paul says that he will show us "a more excellent way". The more "excellent way" is the way of charity and love. As God's people, we should relate to each other from a spirit of love.

Walking in the Spirit

The church cannot function in self-righteousness; we must function in the Spirit of God. God calls us, first out of darkness and then into His marvelous light (I Peter 2:9). So many Christians experience great peace and are able to walk steadily with God. But when we take our focus off God, the peace slips away and we struggle in our fleshly emotions. When the Spirit of God is quenched, the person will often slip back into the practice of finding satisfaction from fleshly desires. He or she imitates the life of the Spirit and it converts to "empty works" (no validity to God)

God needs us to be free from failure and through Him we can be. To stay away from failure, we must yield to God in obedience whether we feel like it or not. This is not an easy thing to do, especially if one is dealing with strongholds and issues that have not been submitted to God. But we must set our minds on the things above. We must set our minds like we set our clocks; on time. We must be diligent in preparation for worship and in the participation of it. God will fulfill His part, but we must fulfill our part by making the Bible the ultimate authority in our lives and make God our priority. We can choose to walk in the authority of the Spirit of God and not in the works of the flesh.

Chapter 7

The Power in Releasing Burdens

"It is for freedom that Christ has set us free. Stand firm, then and do not let yourselves be burdened again by a yoke of slavery."

(Galatians 5:1)

Sleeping with holiness is completely dying to self, walking in the spirit, and being completely intimate with God. We must leave self-effort, self-centeredness and self-destruction out of our equation for total dependence on God. So what does this mean? We must allow God through his Holy Spirit to carry the purpose in our lives. If we are struggling with our purpose on earth, then there is unease in our spirits. There is a hindrance in allowing the Holy Spirit to flow freely in our lives. Nothing good can come of exercising our own will.

It is the good that comes from the indwelling power and spirit of God which provides us with the daily necessities. He teaches us how to discern, how to fight, how to pray, how to worship, how to listen and how to be still. We must learn how to commit to our cross without staggering back and forth between confusion and confidence. Once we are committed to the cross, then our hearts can receive God's deliverance, healing, everlasting joy, and the peace that will sustain us through every storm.

We must lay aside all of our self-righteousness, self-pride, self-will, selfishness, anger, hurt, stubbornness, lust and greed. We must take it off, leave it at the altar, and continue to seek God's counsel. God has so many things to reveal to those who choose not to compromise or conform to the culture of this world. God will bring us closer to Him and expose the truth about who we really are and what His will is for us. But we cannot turn back to drinking, drugging, fornication or promiscuity. Freedom comes with a price. It may require giving up family relationships that keeps you from growing in Christ.

The moment Christ died, was buried, resurrected from the dead, and ascended back to heaven, God freed us from the burdens of affliction, pain and suffering. We may find ourselves carrying a load of burdens for people at church, our families and even for ourselves. Even in these situations, we are expected to release the weight into the hand of God and keep pressing forward.

Burdens are described as a heaviness or obligation of the mind, heart and soul. Some burdens can be destructive or come from God, sent as a divine message of intercession or warning. Burdens impact our cognitive, spiritual and physiological focus.

In order to be released from the yoke of oppression, as believers, we must submit these burdens to God and trust in the way He chooses to handle them. God's divine power manifests itself from the spiritual world to the earth by means of our fervent ongoing prayer, fasting and faith. Though we may not always see it or feel it immediately, God makes His power accessible to us on earth. Yet we sometimes lack spiritual understanding on how to use divine power for a breakthrough.

Galatians 5:1 says to "*Stand firm*", the body of Christ has been made free. Yes, it is difficult to "stand' when the cares of life wear us down and there seems to be no way to escape. But we are free from bearing the weight of pain, the weight of financial burdens, the weight of sickness, and the weight of uncertainty. All we have to do is trust, let go and surrender our burdens to the Lord.

Communication with God

Prayer is communication between God and man. Prayer keeps our fellowship with God active and fresh. Prayer is not a conduit to request material gains. It is a lifestyle choice, an ongoing exchange between our creator and the spirit man. Through prayer, we can tap into the supernatural to cast down, tear down, destroy yokes, build up and maintain protection. We must develop our spirits to thirst and hunger for prayer.

During joyous moments or even times of trouble, it is important to develop a hunger to seek and hear the voice of God for correction and instruction. Maintaining a strong prayer life is critical because the works of the flesh are in opposition to the desires of our spirit man. Our humanness sucks the breath out of our prayer life, breaking bridges of communication with God. The nature of our flesh has a different perspective on our prayer life. The flesh becomes distracted and bored easily. It takes away from effective and fervent prayer by wanting to follow its own agenda.

Sometimes, after we pray for a particular situation or person, the burden will not always be removed from our mind. We call this Satan's strategic plan of diversion. Our hearts get released from the burden but our minds struggle to separate from it. Satan uses the power of guilt to consume our peace about that situation. But Paul says in 2 Corinthians: 10:5 to cast down imaginations; come out of agreement with that thing that is afflicting your mind. We must continue to meditate on this verse at least two or three times per day and demand our peace. Satan must loose our minds from the power of torment. God will provide peace in our hearts, peace in our minds and peace in our bodies! Believe it and then wait on it.

A Time of Sacrifice

In the old testament, there were demonstrations of effective fasting and the delivery of divine communication. Daniel devoted his time for 21 days of fasting, praying, and making supplications unto the Lord (Daniel 10:2-3). In the 21st century, we are living under hard times; people face financial burdens, unsaved children, broken marriages, infirmities and evil strongholds in our households and churches. This is the season of release for a holy revival where power is rejuvenated; burdens will be lifted up, minds will be freed, bodies will be healed and financial breakthroughs will occur.

God is calling for a season of prayer and fasting for the corporate body and individuals. Again, we must stress the importance of fasting and prayer. Jesus told His disciples that *"This kind can come forth by nothing, but by prayer and fasting."* (Mark 9:29) Prayer and fasting is an important part of a Christian's life. It aids us in deliverance and healing. We must practice prayer and fasting regularly to overcome the fiery darts of the enemy.

For most of us, if it is up to our circumstances, we would never find a good time to fast, especially when our schedules are consumed by a 40-hour work week and activities at home. Despite these busy lives and external limitations, God calls for incessant prayer and consistently disciplined spirits anchored with fasting.

The principle of fasting is one of God's ways to release His power in our lives. Fasting is another element in the Christian lifestyle that draws us closer to God and develops spiritual maturity. Fasting is not intended to be punitive; it's a pleasure and an opportunity to experience God's power, to renounce worldly regiments, be released from burdens, receive supernatural healing, and have financial blessings; all of which are added to generations to come. Though our situation may not change, fasting changes us; our perception, our bad habits, and our negative response to situations.

Activating Our Faith

Hebrews 11:1 says, *"Now faith is the substance of things hoped for, the evidence of things not seen."* God is refining and maturing our faith through tests and trials. There is hardship in our lives often in order to build our faith.

At times, we may have a certain portion of faith sitting dormant within our lives. It often will not become active until challenges occur. Our biggest challenge is to see these experiences as a conduit to release our faith.

Why do we fail to release our faith? Fear works against the grain of faith. As a result, we look for answers in the wrong places. Instead of trusting God, there is a continuous attempt to figure out our problems the familiar way and as best as we can without relying on divine intervention from the Holy Spirit. There is a disconnection between letting go of our burdens (surrendering) and believing the truth about God's word (faith).

God has an immeasurable timeframe to respond to our prayers. We must stop trying to figure it all out because we can't. We cannot do it all by ourselves. We must be patient for it, pray on it, fast and keep on waiting for God's release. But when God tells us to move, then we must move. We must not wait another minute or a second after we hear from Him. We must take our eyes off our circumstances, activate our faith and trust God. If God is faithful, then we must be faithful. We must walk by faith, not by sight (2 Corinthians 5:7).

Why Resilience?

Resilience is critically important for coping with the wears and tears of life. Resilience is not attained only by what we've experienced, but by how we overcome the challenges in those experiences, and the tenacity with which we struggle against these painful battles.

We are chosen by God, a generation clothed with strength and humility, to deal with the woes of life; struggles, adversities and relationship conflict. There is a level of resilience needed to move into our next spiritual plane. Resilience is in us. Past limitations and hostile environments cannot hurt our future. We are children of the Most High God with the power to tread upon serpents and scorpions. Nothing and no one can stop us from receiving God's healing and deliverance power. That painful childhood experience has given you purpose. If Satan had the power to kill you in that situation, he would have already killed you.

We must not let our past haunt us. Talk about it, release it to God and then let it go. If we don't, Satan will steal our emotions and play with them like a batch of dough. The enemy will remove our focus from God and eventually we lose our fasting and prayer life. Negative emotions will settle in our souls. A person who experience chronic depression lacks resilience, anxiety lacks resilience and fear lacks resilience. These stressful events make us vulnerable to the cycle of fleshly works. However, there is an ongoing spiritual battle to restore our minds, hearts and spirits.

When we call on the matchless, marvelous and majestic name of Jesus, the Holy Spirit will intervene and God will know our thoughts. We must reconcile our faith; examine God's promises for our lives by reading and mediating on His Word and seek God's power, meaning and purpose in our lives. It's time to renew our strength. It's time to examine our thoughts, ways and attitudes. Instead of asking God: why we went through what we went through, we should ask God what does He want us to get out of this situation.

After a successful and God filled 14-year marriage with two children, God called my husband home to be with Him in 2009. My life and the life of my children changed expeditiously. The head of our household was gone. My companion and best friend was gone. Since I was several months behind in payments, my mortgage was in the process of modification. Decision making, roles and positions within the household shifted. However, my zeal for God grew stronger. My relationship with God (prayer life, fasting and faith) grew stronger. In the midst of my storm, I still found strength and power in God to minister to others in need.

Through rough seasons God shows us what we are made of. There is no greater goal than to develop stronger resilience to prepare for our next level, next battle and new assignment. Where there is purpose and growth, there is pain also. For unto whomsoever much is given, of him shall be much required. (Luke12:48 KJV). This is the season for our reward, our breakthrough, our blessing. Get ready for the change that is inevitable.

"Neither do men pour new wine into old wineskins". Matthew 9:17. Negative attitudes and traditional practices have no place in the new season. Something must be released in order for freedom to take place. When we release old feelings or past hurts, we have to take on a new character; this develops resilience. Resilience gives us a fresh start because it allows us to spring back from divorce, sickness, unemployment, foreclosure or loss of a loved one.

Grape vine varieties have intense resilience to the many things that can damage them. Our resilience comes directly from the True Vine, which is Christ Jesus. Through resilience, we learn to respond to disappointments, failures, grief, loss and obstacles in the way Christ would respond. Building intimate relationship with God and other believers who are supportive will help us develop resilience.

Chapter 8

Counting the Cost of Holiness

"Then I looked on all the works that my hands had wrought, and on the labour that it had cost me to do them; and behold, all was vanity and pursuit of the wind, and there was no profit under the sun."

(Ecclesiastes 2:11)

Believers once lived secular lives, but we accepted a new way of living in holiness through Christ Jesus. We proclaimed and committed to the faith. Once we've counted the cost of holiness, we can and must persevere until the end of our time. We often wonder what or how much more will it cost?

Whenever there is a gain in life there is also the other side of the coin which requires us to give up, suffer, or sacrifice something. Holiness mandates us to be valuable in the kingdom of God. Because of it, we are persecuted for our standards, our Savior, and our stand. Holiness requires us to give up bad attitudes, some relationships, self-righteousness, the world's approval, resentment and bitterness. It causes us to walk in humility. Through the process of denying ourselves, we must learn from it, grow in it, and move forward through it.

It is important to count the cost of holiness because it will help us to remain focused. Many Christians build good ministries for the kingdom of God. Along the way however, they end up accepting benefits for themselves and building themselves up. King Solomon, for example, had many wives and his wealth was enormous. He was renowned throughout the nations for his wisdom and his wealth. He began to live for pleasures instead of living for God. In 1 Kings 11:9-13, the Lord punished Solomon by tearing the kingdoms in two because his heart turned away from God by marrying foreign women and worshipping their gods. God wasn't pleased then and God isn't pleased now with idol worship in the body of Christ today. We must be committed to worshipping God and God alone.

It is a blessing to have and remain in covenant with God because He will always provide for us. Christians who chose to step out of holiness have lost rights and privileges to the blessings of God. God wants us to operate with kingdom principles. He wants us to continue to embrace His righteousness as we walk in His ways. He wants to shower us with blessings. God understands it is challenging to be righteous and to remain committed in difficult times. But we have freedom to choose. We can either give up or remain faithful until the end. We must weigh the cost of holiness!

We are to embrace all that we go through for righteousness sake and not give in to our fleshly nature for pleasure or comfort. Even when we miss the mark and sin, we can get back in our good standing with God through repentance. How do we know when we are far away from God? The Bible says, *"Let a man examine himself."* (1 Corinthians 11:28). We need to examine ourselves just like Solomon did. Solomon looked *"On all the works that my hands had wrought, and on the labour that it had cost"* (vs.11a). Solomon was so caught up in himself but he had a choice to continue in sin or to repent, turn back to God and yield himself to holiness.

Today, we have the same choice as Solomon. When we push our holiness to the sidelines, our eyes will eventually become dim to our purpose for God. What do we really profit under the sun? Solomon profited his wives, wealth, and wisdom, but he lost focus on his purpose. His profits were not beneficial to the kingdom of God because he sacrificed his holiness instead of his self-righteousness.

The beauty of holiness is that we will always find the Lord. His presence will remain and dwell with us and the fruit of our lives will be a magnification of Him. The beauty of Holiness is that it does offer benefits to believers; it prepares us for heaven, sanctifies our souls, gives us freedom in our hearts and transforms. We cannot operate in sanctity without it.

Persecution for Our Standards

The price of holiness often results in persecution for our standards. If and when this happens, it lets us know that we are in the right position and on the right track. Jesus said, *"If they have persecuted me, they will persecute you."* (John 15:20). Persecution is a part of the world's behavior towards believers. As followers of Christ we can expect to be persecuted also.

As a Christian, our standards, based on the Word, shape our decision, identify who we belong to, and show who we are. The world often despises us for it because by doing "good" and living like Christ, it exposes their wrong. We know that sometimes it is very difficult to understand how to put God's principles into practice, especially when the world treats us badly. But the holiness of God will lead us to love, forgiveness and reconciliation.

We make decisions everyday based on either worldly viewpoint or the righteousness of God. In Genesis 22:1-13, Abraham was commanded by God to sacrifice his son Isaac. As a father and a man of God, Abraham had the choice to either protect his son from death as a father is expected to or adhere to righteousness by obeying the command of God. If the center of our strength is Christ Jesus, then what are our standards? What do we base our decisions on?

Abraham's strength was in his obedience to God. His decision was an incredibly difficult one but, *"he believed in the LORD; and he counted it to him for righteousness."* (Genesis 15:6). Christians must understand that our principles, practices, and ways of life make us different from others around us. We, as born again believers, should not share the same values and ways, patterns, or perception of this world. We should see God's grace as sufficient, His love as our strength and His power perfected in our weakness (2 Corinthians 12:9-10).

Persecution for Our Savior

When we are persecuted for living a holy life, then we must count it all joy! Jesus consoles us with these words, *"In my Father's house are many mansions: if it were not so, I would have told you. I go to prepare a place for you."*(John 14:2) It is a joy to know that even through persecutions, we have a steady place in Jesus.

The world speculates on our love and faithfulness for Christ Jesus. They question our faith in Him. If we are insulted because of Jesus, we can consider ourselves truly blessed. If our family and friends forsake us because of our love for Christ, then we are in God's perfect will. Our strength lies first and foremost in our Lord and Savior Jesus Christ. He not only leads, but also brings victory to every battle for us. Jesus has already set the paths that we should walk while on earth.

David reassures us that, *"I have been young, and now am old; yet have I not seen the righteous forsaken, nor his seed begging bread."* (Psalm 37:25). God taught us through Christ Jesus to persevere in our tribulations because He is our provision. He has never let us suffer, except it be for righteousness. Through our stand for Christ, we will receive an abundance of joy, peace, love, power, and most of all eternal life. All these come from the unceasing and undying authority of Christ Jesus. Jesus knew that we would face persecutions (see Matthew 5:10-11). He prepares our hearts with logos and rhema, the written and spoken word of God.

As Christians, we don't want to wander deeper into woods of life and be blinded to the path of righteousness. It can lead us to emptiness and void our purpose. It will result in despair. Depression will meet us at the road of apostasy. If we give in to apostasy, God will give us up to our own weaknesses to show us how much we need Him (Romans 1:26). Only when we cease to live for ourselves and live solely for Christ Jesus, can we see the full purpose of holiness. We will then be able to rejoice because *"In him we live, and move, and have our being"* (Acts 17:28). It is so great to be on the Lord's side!

Persecution for Our Stand

After you have done all that you can do, just stand. Stand in the righteousness of God despite oppositions, despite your afflictions, despite disappointments and despite your losses. The world finds it impossible to stand in righteousness when trouble comes their way. They do not understand how believers remain confident in the Lord even while we experience trials and tribulations. God has given us the armor to be able to withstand in the evil days (Ephesian 6:10-17). True believers do not divert in their stand when facing tribulations. We persevere with praises and thanksgiving to our heavenly Father. Holiness keeps us steadfast and immovable. And therefore, we are able to stay committed to God in spite of the personal cost.

The world delights to see a child of God err in his or her ways. We must not allow anyone or any circumstance to hinder us from pursuing holiness. We must continue to pray and encourage those who are facing persecution and temptation. If we are to have victory and prosperity all the way through the end times, then we must utilize the entire armor of God. When we do all that we can do, God blesses and upholds us, and we can stand until the very end.

One of the greatest strengths for Christians in their stand against the world is to experience God's presence consistently. Being in the presence of God is one cost to holiness. God speaks and guide us when we abide in His presence. As we spend time in God's presence, His character manifests in our attitudes, in our thoughts, and in the way we respond to our circumstances. We want His presence to follow us wherever we go.

Sometimes we become so busy, focused on ourselves or frustrated that we don't spend enough time with God. Days go by and then weeks and months. We will notice the emptiness in our worship and develop a feeble stand for God. God desires to have fellowship with every one of His children. He wants us to give ourselves entirely to Him so in spite of persecution so He can deposit strength in us as we commune with Him. He wants us to stay firm in our stand for Him.

The Furnace Experience

Every now and then, we come against the fiery trials that produce fire. Some people fear the furnace experience because of the afflictions and pain they must endure. But God uses fire to loose us from the rope that spiritually ties us down. He uses fire to burn all impurities away so that we can operate in this world effectively for Him. There will be furnaces of trials, furnaces of fears, furnaces of disappointments, furnaces of temptation, and furnaces of criticism. But as long as we look to Jesus, nothing by any

73

means shall harm us. The furnaces of life have no pleasure for us but once we stand through them with Jesus on our side, it is worth the costs.

What happens in us during the furnace fire is much more important than what happens to us during the fire. As we go through it, we become more holy like Jesus. Just as gold and silver are purified through the fiery process, the furnace fire in our lives removes the impurities. The more He purifies us, the more holy we become. When God sends us through a small furnace and His outcome is achieved, He will place us in a greater furnace to continue the process of refinement. The greater the pain, the greater the anointing.

There's no need to fear because God's people are preserved by His holiness. He will see us through. We are graced by God and He will perfect His children. God sees the excellence in us. He wants to promote us in His perfect plan! He desires to take us to a new level of holiness, peace, joy, productiveness and fulfillment. God will advance us because of our faithfulness. When God sends us through the furnace, we will mature in character. It will not harm us, but grow us. He will send us there because He will use our lives in a great way. We must remain faithful no matter what! God sealed every believer with the covenant through the blood of Jesus.

We pray you will find greater peace and comfort in the fact that God has your best interest at heart. He knows us and loves us and wants only the best for us. Regardless of our past or current circumstances, be encouraged to follow Jesus with all diligence and faithfulness. As we do, God will turn around our finances, reconcile relationships, expand ministries, and so on.

If you are passing through a furnace today, hold fast to God's unchanging hand. He is with you in your furnace and He will bring you through it. You must face persecutions on earth for being a child of the Most High. God has been with you through every left and wrong turn. Choose this day who you will serve, a faithful God who is eternal or the world that will soon perish.

The altar of repentance is open. Talk to Jesus and tell him all about your furnaces! Jesus is saying, *"Cast thy burden upon the LORD, and he shall sustain thee: he shall never suffer the righteous to be moved."* (Psalm 55:22). It's time for the true worshippers to draw closer in fellowship and intimacy with God. The end result is worth the cost!

"And that, knowing the time, that now it is high time to awake out of sleep: for now is our salvation nearer than when we believe. The night is far spent, the day is at hand: let us therefore cast off the works of darkness, and let us put on the armour of light. Let us walk honestly, as in the day; not in rioting and drunkenness, not in chambering and wantonness, not in strife and envying. But put ye on the Lord Jesus Christ, and make not provision for the flesh, to fulfil the lusts thereof." (Romans 13:11-14)

Prayers

We would like to close with two prayers: one is for the unsaved who has never confessed Jesus as their Lord and Savior, but desire to do so. The second prayer is for every believer. We want to encourage you to keep the faith and endure to the end.

Sinners Prayer for the unbelievers

As you say this prayer, God will dispatch his heavenly angels to protect and guide you through your purpose. Continue to walk in your trials and tribulations. Romans 10:9 say, "that if thou shall confess with thy mouth the Lord Jesus, and shalt believe in thy heart that God hath raised him from the dead, thou shalt be saved.

Father God, I have sinned against you and I am heartily sorry. Please forgive me and save my soul from eternal death. I believe that your son Jesus died for me and you have raised him from the dead. Rest, rule, and abide in me so I can live free. I choose to serve you and only you until the day of Jesus Christ's return. Thank you for my salvation. In Jesus name. Amen!

We welcome you to the Body of Christ Jesus! Now begin to praise God for his underserving love and dunamis power!

Prayer for the believers

Heavenly Father, We pray for the awakening of your sons and daughters. We pray that every believer will rest in your sovereignty and learn to trust you during high and low seasons. Awake your children with the fire to burn away their past and present afflictions, (addiction, stealing, lying, jealousy, etc.). Awake them with the anointing power to conquer every adversity and challenges in their lives. We pray that your sons and daughters will (re-)commit himself/ herself to a life of consecration, life of peace and life of humility to manage through their tribulations. You have not called them to compromise, but to tread on serpents and scorpions that enter into their path. You have not given them the spirit of fear, but of power, and of love, and of a sound mind to rest in you. We thank you in advance for their deliverance, their healing, and a closer walk with you. We thank you for being a faithful and merciful God. We thank you for your grace. We pray in your Son Jesus' name. Amen!

Everyone: Now unto him that is able to keep you from falling, and to present you faultless before the presence of his glory with exceeding joy, To the only wise God our Saviour, be glory and majesty, dominion and power, both now and ever. Amen. (Jude 1:24-25)

Author's Bio

Twin sisters, Daura Jones and Daphne Parker are founders of Two Hearts for Children and Family Services of New York, Inc, a 501c3 federally tax exempt organization.

In response to a cry from the children of God living in New York City, Two Hearts has launched its mentoring program for children between the ages of 5 years to 18 years infected/affected by HIV/AIDS or who live in single parent head of household.

Our mission is to empower, stabilize and expand the resource capacity of individuals and families to become self-sufficient in their lives.

We strive to reduce the causes and characteristics of poverty and otherwise assist persons in need by providing direct support, working in partnership with communities and other agencies to provide a range of human, educational and economic development to services.

For more information about our programs, volunteer opportunities or if you would like to financially support our organization, please email us at: twoheartsny@gmail.com.